English Together

Action Book 2

Diana Webster and Anne Worrall

Unit 1

A **Ask your class.**

Where were your friends in the holidays?
Ask six friends.

A: Where were you in the holidays? **B: I was by the sea.**

Write the names. Tick (✓) the answers.

name	at home	by the sea	in the mountains	in the country
1				
2				
3				
4				
5				
6				

E.T. Write about you and your friends in
your ET book.

In the holidays I was...

My friend Alissia was...

B **Read and write.**

What's wrong? Write the sentences again.

1 A T-shirt is wearing Emma.

<u>Emma is wearing a T-shirt.</u>

2 A fish is eating the cat.

_____

3 The horses are feeding Al and Beth.

_____

4 A house is sitting on a bird.

_____

5 A table is running under a spider.

_____

6 A tree is climbing a bear.

_____

C **Colour and write.**

red	☐	twenty	20	twelve	☐	orange	☐
thirteen	☐	blue	☐	fifty	☐	eighty	☐
green	☐	a hundred	☐	thirty	☐	brown	☐
nineteen	☐	yellow	☐	pink	☐	seven	☐

D Listen. Write the numbers on the photos.

E Write.

Answer the questions.

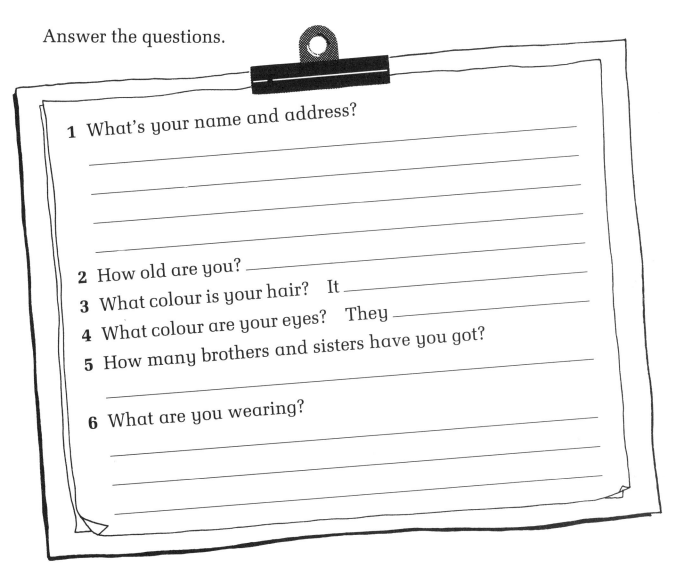

1 What's your name and address?

_____

_____

_____

2 How old are you? _____

3 What colour is your hair?   It _____

4 What colour are your eyes?   They _____

5 How many brothers and sisters have you got?

_____

6 What are you wearing?

_____

_____

_____

Now ask your partner.
Write the answers in your ET book.

Draw your partner's picture and colour it.

My partner's name is Anna.
Her address is...

Unit 2

A Write *this* or *that*.

1 Who's __this__?
It's my uncle.

2 Who's __that__?
My aunt.

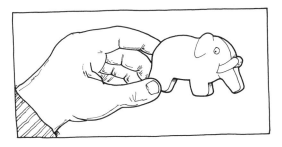

3 What's _____?
A rubber.

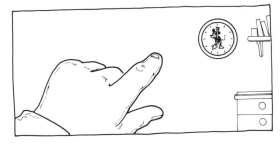

4 What's _____?
It's a clock.

5 Is _____ your book?
Yes.

6 Is _____ your bike?
No, it's my brother's.

7 _____'s my school.

8 _____ is my dog.

B Look and write.

There are two ghosts in the castle.
They are friends. What do they do
every day? Choose from here:

sing	open	sit
watch TV	draw	read
write	dance	close

1 Every day the two ghosts
dance.

2 And they _____.

3 The white ghost _opens_
doors.

4 The black ghost _____
windows.

5 The ghosts _____ in
chairs and _____ books.

6 The white ghost _____ on
the wall.

7 The black ghost _____
pictures.

8 And at twelve o'clock the two
ghosts _____.

C Listen and say.

On Monday alone,
On Tuesday together,
On Wednesday we walk
In windy weather.
On Thursday we climb,
On Friday we run,
And on Saturday and Sunday,
We play and have fun.

D Listen and write.

Look at the pictures.

Listen and tick (✔) the picture.

Write about one picture.

Picture

_____

_____

_____

E Ask your class.

Write the questions.

Have you got an uncle?

How many uncles have you got?

_____ an aunt?

How many _____?

_____ cousin?

How _____?

Now ask four friends.

	name	uncles	aunts	cousins
1				
2				
3				
4				

F A letter. Listen and read.

Dear Beth,
My name is Mitsuko Hashimoto. I live in Kyoto, Japan. I am nine. I have got a brother and a sister. My brother's name is Hitoshi. He is eleven. My sister's name is Kyomi. She is nearly four.
I like animals. I have got a cat. Her name is Yoko.
I can skateboard and I can swim well, too.
Please write and send a photo.
                    Yours,
                        Mitsuko

This is me, Mitsuko

Write a letter to Mitsuko in your ET book about you.

Unit 3

A Write.

Yesterday I (clean) _cleaned_ my room. Then I (wash) _____ the dishes. Then I (go) _____ to the shops. Then I (play) _____ with a friend. We (listen) _____ to music and we (play) _____ a game. Then I (watch) _____ TV with my family. I (go) _____ to bed at nine o'clock.

B Read and write.

What's happening in the pictures? Look and write the number.

☐ Emma is opening the door.	☐ Cleo is opening the cupboard. `1`
☐ The door is closing.	☐ Cleo is miaowing.
☐ Cleo is happy.	☐ She is going in.

What happened? Tell the story. Write.
Cleo opened the cupboard. Then she...
_____
_____

10

C **Listen and draw.**

up ↑ down ↓

Listen to Joe's story and draw a line.

P.B.
p.17

D **Play a game.**

Draw the animals in the rooms in your picture:

1 spiders   **2** a cat   **3** a dog   **4** bats   **5** snakes   **6** a bird   **7** frogs

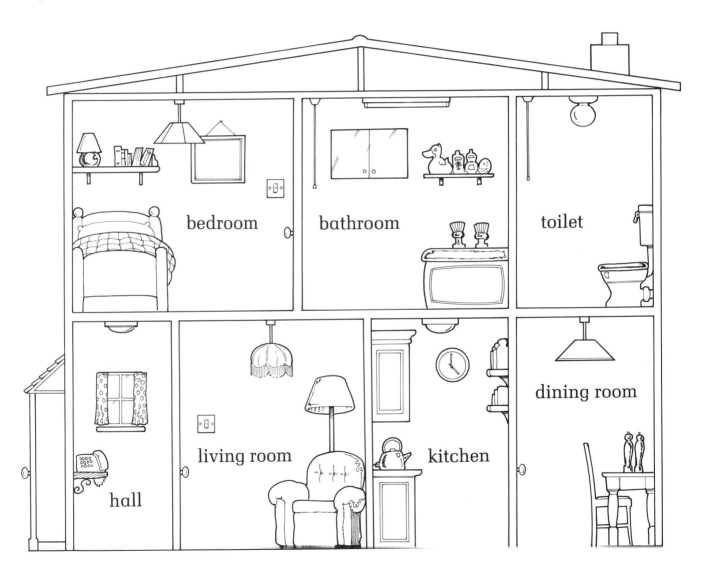

bedroom   bathroom   toilet

dining room

living room   kitchen

hall

Partner **A**, look at **B**'s picture. Then don't look.
Where were the animals in **B**'s picture? Can you
remember? Ask and answer. Take it in turns.

E Look and write.

What animal was number **1**? Where was it?

Number **1** _was a_ _____ It was _____

Number **2** _____

Number **3** _____

Number **4** _____

Number **5** _____

F Find and write.

How many rooms can you find?

h	o	l	h	k	b	e	d	d	l
c	i	t	c	h	a	l	l	i	i
t	e	o	l	i	t	a	i	n	v
c	k	i	t	c	h	e	n	m	i
h	o	l	i	v	r	t	d	i	n
e	b	e	d	r	o	o	m	e	g
b	u	t	h	r	o	h	a	l	r
i	k	c	r	o	m	l	e	t	o
e	y	h	o	o	m	b	a	t	o
d	i	n	i	n	g	r	o	o	m

kitchen, _____

_____

_____

13

Unit 4

A Listen and tick the answers.

Four children are talking. What do they want to do?

Tom					
Sara					
Maria					
Tony					

 What does Tom want to do? And Sara? Write in your ET book.

B Write *this* or *these*.

You and Tim are looking at a family photo.
Tim:

__This__ is my grandma.
__These__ are my aunts.
_____ is my uncle.
_____ is my father.
_____ are my cousins.
_____ is my mother.
_____ are my brothers.
And _____ is me!

14

C Write the questions.

1 What __did__ Beth press?
   She pressed the keys.

2 What _____ she __type__?
   She typed her name.

3 What game _____ she choose?
   She chose 'Space'.

4 What _____ she _____ then?
   She picked up the black box.

5 Where _____ the children _____?
   They stood in the circle.

6 What _____ Beth _____ then?
   She pressed the red button.

7 Where _____?
   They were in a spaceship.

D Choose the odd one out.

aunt	
uncle	
(witch)	
cousin	
__mother__	

England
Scotland
Tuesday
Wales
_____

kitchen
bathroom
toilet
planet
_____

shoe
knife
cup
fork
_____

sweater
short
hat
dress
_____

hair
nose
rice
ear
_____

Write a new word in the boxes.

15

E **Read and write.**

You are playing a computer game. There is a big castle . . .

The computer says this: What did you do?

Go into the castle.

Look at the table.

Pick up a key.

Open a door.

Close the door.

Go down the stairs.

Go into a room.

Open a box.

Pick up a ring.

I went into the castle.

_____

_____

_____

_____

_____

_____

_____

Well done! You've got the magic ring!

F **Write *do*, *does* or *did*.**

1 **Does** Emma like horses?   No, she likes cats.

2 What _____ Beth like?   She likes horses.

3 What _____ Beth do yesterday?   She played a game.

4 Where _____ Beth, Joe and Tammy go?   They went in a spaceship.

5 What _____ you do yesterday?

(Write the answer) _____

G **Read and write the number on the pictures.**

1 This game is about two boys and a girl. They are playing on a beach. They find a bottle on the beach. It has got a letter in it. They read the letter and go to an old castle. What happens then? Wait and see!

2 Two girls and a boy are playing in a castle. They find an old box. They open the box and see a ring. It is a magic ring. Where do they go? What do they do? Watch the video and see!

3 Two boys, a girl and a dog are playing on the beach. The dog finds a huge cave. In the cave there is a black box. The children open the box and find treasure! But two men see the children and the treasure . . .

Give the three videos a name. Here are two names. Make up one name.

The secret letter

The magic ring

A Write *That is* or *Those are*.

You are on the new planet. What can you see?

1 <u>That is</u> a rainbow.   **2** <u>Those are</u> flowers.   **3** _____ mushrooms.

4 _____ butterfly.   **5** _____ bees.   **6** _____ mice.

B Make a rhyme.

Listen and choose from here:

fat	thin	old	young	short	tall

Mr Hall is very _____.

Mrs Port is very _____.

Miss Sprat is very _____.

Ms Sin is very _____.

Mr Gold is very _____.

And Tommy Sung is very _____.

Then read the rhyme. Can you make up new names?

C **Ask and answer.**

What did you and your partner have when you were six? What were you afraid of?
Write the questions.

	Yes	No
1 Did you have a pet?		
2 _____ you have a computer?		
3 _____ have a teddy bear?		
4 _____ a doll?		
5 Were you afraid of spiders?		
6 _____ afraid of big dogs?		

Ask your partner. Tick the answers.

E.T. In your ET book, write about your partner like this:

When my friend Sara
was six, she had a pet.
It was a cat. She
didn't have a computer.
She had a teddy bear
and a doll. She was
afraid of spiders. She
wasn't afraid of big
dogs.

Then write about you.

19

D Read and write the numbers.

What did they have for tea on the spaceship? Write the numbers.

 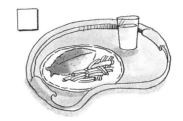 

1 Tammy didn't have fish. She had two sausages and salad. She didn't have coffee – she had milk.

2 Joe had two sausages and chips. He didn't have salad. He had milk, but he didn't have coffee.

3 Beth didn't have sausages. She had fish and chips. She had salad, too. She didn't have milk.

Number **4** is Cleo's tea. What did she have? Write in your ET book:

Cleo had...

E Questions and answers.

Can you remember the story?
Look at the questions. Then find the answer and write the number.

1 Where were Beth, Joe, Tammy and Cleo?   ☐ They saw giant flowers and mushrooms.

2 Did Tammy see a car?   ☐ No, she saw a satellite.

3 Did they land on the moon?   **1** They were in a spaceship.

4 What did they see on the planet?   ☐ No, she was afraid.

5 Did Cleo like the mice?   ☐ No, they landed on a planet.

F Listen and tick the answers.

1 What did they see on the Earth?

☐ Africa   ☐ India   ☑ Australia

2 What colour was the new planet?

☐ blue   ☐ green   ☐ yellow   ☐ red   ☐ orange

3 What was the planet like?

☐   ☐   ☐

4 What time did they land on the planet?

☐   ☐   ☐

5 What did they see on the planet?

☐   ☐   ☐

6 What was the weather like?

☐ hot   ☐ cold

7 What else did they see?

☐ a car   ☐ a rainbow   ☐ a mouse   ☐ a spaceship

G Write.

Write about a new planet in your ET book. What was it like? What did you see? Draw a picture.

Unit 6

A **Write the words.**

Uncle Colin's machines can go wrong. What happened yesterday? Choose from here:

| make | pick up | clean | wash | paint | take |

1 This machine ___makes___ the beds, __but__ yesterday it ___made___ Uncle Colin!

2 This machine _____ your back, _____ yesterday it _____ Joe's face.

3 This machine _____ the room, _____ yesterday it _____ Beth.

4 This machine _____ the dog for a walk, _____ yesterday it _____ Al for a walk.

5 This machine _____ the windows, _____ yesterday it _____ Cleo.

6 This machine _____ paper, _____ yesterday it _____ Tammy.

22

B Look and write.

These were Al's jobs today.

✓	wash the dishes
	make my bed
✓	clean my room
	go to the shops
✓	do my homework
	wash my hair

What did he do? What didn't he do?

He washed the dishes but he didn't make his bed.

C Listen to some English children. Write.

P.B. p.31

	John	Sara	Anna	James
1 Where does he/she live?				
In the town.	✓			
In the country.				
2 What is his/her home like?				
It's a house.				
It's a flat.	✓			
3 Is it big?	Yes			
4 How many bedrooms are there?	2			
5 Has it got a garden?	No			

D Listen and say the rhyme.

In a town there was an old, old castle.
In the castle there was a big, big room.
In the room there was a tall, tall cupboard.
In the cupboard there was a small, small box.
In the box there was a tiny, tiny . . .

GHOST!

E A puzzle.

Write the words and answer the question.

1 You can wear it.
2 You can fly in it.
3 Kangaroos live here.
4 You sit on it.
5 You see with it.
6 It's in the sky. It's hot.
7 You can ride on it.
8 You can eat it. It's cold.
9 You write with it.

| S | O | C | K |

What is Tammy's birthday present? A _____.

P.B. p.31 **F** **Diaries.**

 your diary

| Monday |
| Tuesday |
| Wednesday |
| Thursday |
| Friday |
| Saturday |
| Sunday |

your partner's diary

| Monday |
| Tuesday |
| Wednesday |
| Thursday |
| Friday |
| Saturday |
| Sunday |

Unit 7

A Look at the chart. Ask and answer.

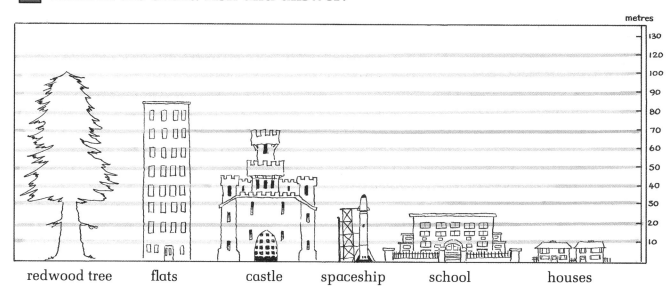

metres
130
120
100
90
80
70
60
50
40
30
20
10

redwood tree   flats   castle   spaceship   school   houses

A: How tall is the redwood tree?   **B:** How tall are the flats?
B: It's a hundred metres tall.   **A:** They're . . .

Now write in your ET books about the redwood tree, the flats, the castle, the spaceship, the school and the houses.

The redwood tree is
a hundred metres
tall.

B Count and write.

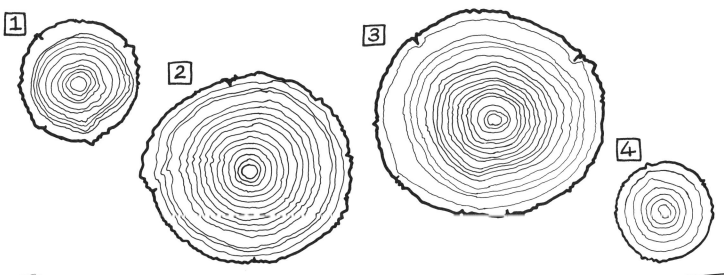

1
2
3
4

How old are the trees? Count and write in your ET books.

1 This tree is
eleven years old.

26

C **Look and listen.**

Joe wants new specs.
He is having an eye test.

Put a tick (✔) in the box when he says the right letter.

Put a cross (✘) in the box when he says the wrong letter.

Now give your friend an eye test. Write ten letters in your ET book. Write two big letters, two small letters, two very small letters and four tiny letters. Can your friend read them?

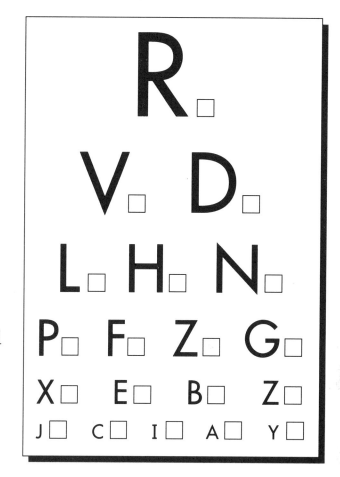

D **Ask your partner.**

Partner **B**, close your book. Partner **A**, ask questions.

Partner **A**

planet
spider
brilliant
happy
summer

Partner **B**

small
address
satellite
holiday
rubber

A: How do you spell 'Planet'?
Has it got one 'n' or two?

A joke
Anna: How do you spell 'wrong'?
Mark: r–o–n–g
Anna: That's wrong.
Mark: I know. That's what you wanted!

27

E **Look and write.**

What do these signs mean?

1 <u>Don't play football here.</u> 2 _____

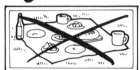
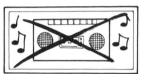

3 _____ 4 _____

_____

play football	listen to music
have a picnic	take your dog for a walk

F **Look and say.**

Where did the bear go?

Now write:

<u>The</u> <u>bear</u> <u>went</u> <u>through</u> <u>the</u> <u>lake</u>,
_____ <u>the</u> <u>raft</u>, _____ _____ _____,

_____ _____ _____, _____ _____, _____

_____ _____, _____ _____,

<u>and</u> <u>she</u> <u>had</u> <u>her</u> <u>lunch</u> _____ __ _____.

28

G **Look at the pictures, choose and write.**

Plant a tree!

1 <u>Find a tree seed</u>.

2 _____

3 _____

4 _____

 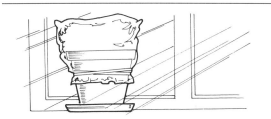

5 _____

6 _____

7 _____
_____

8 _____
_____

Put the pot on a plate.   Put the seed in a pot.
Put the pot in the sun.   Put a plastic bag over the pot.
Find a tree seed.   Water the seed.
The tree is fifteen centimetres tall. Put it in the garden.
You can see a little tree. Take off the bag.

29

A **Look at the pictures, and write.**

What are they going to do?

1 Emma _is going to paint a picture_.

2 Joe and Al _____

3 Beth _____

4 Uncle Colin _____

5 Tammy _____

6 Joe _____

Now ask your partner.

> What are you going to do today?
> What are you going to do on Saturday?

In your ET book write what your partner is going to do after school and on Saturday. Then write what you are going to do today and on Saturday.

B **Look and say.**

What is going to happen?

Now read this:

The cats are going to fly down.
The ghost is going to hide in the
kitchen. The girl is going to step
on the black cat and she's going to
fall up the stairs. The boy is going
to put his foot on the mouse and
the mouse is going to eat the cat.

What's wrong?
Write in your ET book like this:

The cats aren't going
to fly down, the bats
are going to fly down.
The ghost isn't...

31

C Look and write.

These films are in your cinema this week. What films are they?
Choose and write.

1 a cartoon
2 a comedy
3 a musical
4 a horror film
5 an adventure film

Ask your partner.

A: Do you want to see 'Dracula's grandmother'?
B: No, I don't like horror films.
B: Do you want to see 'It's time to laugh'?
A: Yes, I love comedies.

In your ET book write which films you like and which films you don't like.
Then write about your partner in the same way.

D Write questions.

Look at these signs. Write four questions in
your partner's book like this:

When do they feed the bears?

1 _____

2 _____

3 _____

4 _____

Now answer your partner's questions in your ET book.

E Listen and write.

P.B. p.41

Maria   Paul   Adam   Lisa

Listen to the children and tick the chart.

name	doctor	filmstar	pop singer	footballer	teacher
Maria			✓		
Paul					
Adam					
Lisa					

Now write what they are going to be.

Maria is going to be a pop singer.

_____

_____

_____

What are you going to be?

_____

What is your partner going to be?

_____

A joke

Old lady: And how old are you, Mark?
Mark: I'm nine.
Old lady: And what are you going to be?
Mark: Ten!

A Write *it*, *them*, *her* or *him*.

1 Your hands are dirty. Wash **them** , please.

2 Emma is cleaning the car. Help _____ , please.

3 My little brother is hungry. Feed _____ , please.

4 I've got a bike and I can ride _____ .

5 Beth and Al are in the snow. Can you see _____ ?

6 Emma is swimming. Look at _____ .

7 Have you got my socks? I can't find _____ .

8 I want my hat. Have you got _____ ?

B Choose and write.

Look at the picture. Write what the boy is saying and what the girl is saying.

'There is oil on these birds.
Let's take them to that Rescue Centre.'

'Look at those birds.
This Rescue Centre can help them.'

C Look, write and draw.

What are they going to be? Write then finish the pictures.

Picture **1** This is going to be a polar bear.

Picture **2** These are

Picture **3** _____

Picture **4** _____

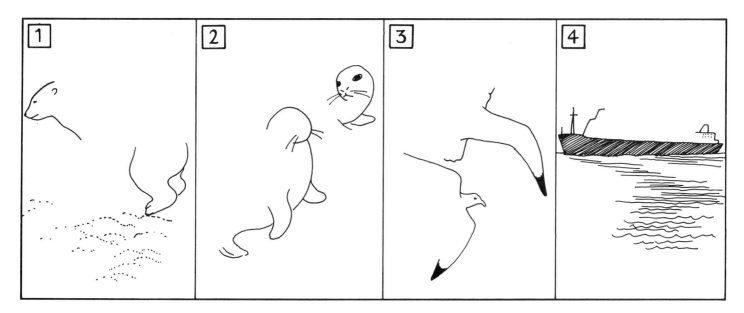

D Choose and write.

Mick and Rick are having a day in the country. What are they saying?
Choose from here:

swim   play   sleep   fish   run   eat

E **Choose and write.**

Because the picture's going to fall on you.
Because I'm going to hide.
Because I'm going to sleep.
Because I'm going to do my homework.
Because we're going to eat our tea.
Because the bear is going to catch you.
Because I'm going to sing.
Because I'm going to feed the seals.

1 Be quiet!
Why?
Because I'm going to sleep.

2 Wash your hands!
Why?

3 Run!
Why?

4 Give me a fish!
Why?

5 Close your eyes!
Why?

6 Put your hands over your ears!
Why?

7 Move!
Why?

8 Give me a pen!
Why?

F **Listen and tick the chart.**

What did they have?

Jenny									✔	
Julie										
John										

Whose litter is in each picture? Write the names.

1

2

3

 G **Game. Clean the beach!**

P.B.
p.47

Spin your spinner and cross out the litter.

How many minutes?

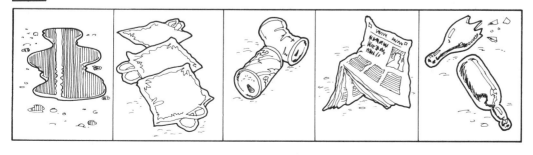

Unit 10

A Listen and write the number plates.

Emma's father's bus.

Joe's mother's car.

Uncle Colin's bike.

Al's mother's car.

Emma's gran's bike.

Tammy's toy car.

B Join the letters in the right order.

What is in the picture? _____

38

C **Find and write.**

Look at this picture. Can you find four things
starting with the letter **s**?
Can you find five things starting with **c**?
And how many things can you find starting with **b**?

s	c	b
snake		

D **Choose and write.**

Emma talked to Uncle Colin about the dungeon.
Uncle Colin asked questions. Here are his
questions. Can you put them in the right places?

Did you open it?
Did you find it there?
Did you find them there?
Did you go down them?
Did you find it there?
Did he open it?

Emma: We looked for the dungeon in the hall . . .

Colin: __Did you find it there?__

Emma: Then we looked for it in the kitchen . . .

Colin: _____

Emma: Joe found a door behind the cupboard . . .

Colin: _____

Emma: We found the stairs . . .

Colin: _____

Emma: We found a box in the dungeon . . .

Colin: _____

Emma: We looked for the diamonds in the box . . .

Colin: _____

Emma: We only found a glass ball!

E **Look and say.**

This is Al's diary for tomorrow.
What is he going to do?

Wednesday

7.00	get up
8.00	swim in the lake
10.00	have breakfast
11.00	feed the dog
12.00	play on the computer

In your ET book, write what Al is
going to do, like this:

Al is going to get up at seven o'clock.		

What are you going to do tomorrow?
Write your diary for tomorrow in your ET book.
Then write what you are going to do.

F **Choose and write.**

I want to see him.   I want to help her.
I want to see her.   He wants to wear them.
I want to listen to it.   She wants to wear it.

Have you got my radio? _I want to listen to it._

Have you got Joe's socks? _____

Is Uncle Colin in the kitchen? _____

Is Emma washing the dog? _____

Have you got Emma's hat? _____

Is Madonna in that film? _____

A Write *our* or *their*.

These children live in Wales. **Their** names are Teg and Evan. _____ father has got a farm and this is _____ sheepdog Kep. They have got a brother and a sister. _____ brother is thirteen and _____ sister is seven.

Teg and Evan: _____ school is very big. There are five hundred children in _____ school. _____ class is big, too. There are thirty-two boys and girls in _____ class. _____ teacher's name is Mrs Cook.

 Write about your school and your friend's school in your ET book.

Our school is ...

B Ask your class.

	name	always	usually	sometimes	no
Do you go to bed late?					
Do you get up early?					
Do you watch TV late?					
Do you work hard?					

 Now write about your friends in your ET book.

C Look and write.

Emma's great-grandfather was a doctor. He had dark hair and a moustache. He wasn't very tall and he wore specs.

Al's great-grandfather was an engineer. He had dark hair and a moustache. He was very tall. He didn't wear specs.

Joe's great-grandfather was a teacher. He wore specs. He had red hair and a red beard.

Whose great-grandfather is picture **A**? _____

Whose great-grandfather is picture **B**? _____

Whose great-grandfather is picture **C**? _____

Ask and answer.

A: Whose great-grandfather had red hair? **B:** Joe's.

E.T. What was your great-grandfather or great-grandmother like? Write in your ET book. Stick in a photo or draw a picture.

My great grandmother was...

43

D Play a game.

Cross off seven things in your squares. Don't show
your partner.

your food and drink

your partner's food and drink

What has your partner got? Partner **A**, ask your
partner for things. Partner **B**, look at your squares
and answer *Yes* or *No*.

Partner **A**, put ticks (✔) or crosses (✘) in **B**'s squares.
Take it in turns. Who can guess five things their partner has got first?

E Listen and tick the answers.

Look at the picture and listen. Right or wrong?

	right	wrong
1	☐	☑
2	☐	☐
3	☐	☐
4	☐	☐
5	☐	☐
6	☐	☐
7	☐	☐

F Write three words in each box.

clothes

jeans
a skirt
_____
_____

food

an ice cream
_____
_____
_____

colours

_____
black
_____
_____

in the kitchen

a plate
_____
_____
_____

at school

_____
_____
a pencil
_____

a face

_____
an eye
_____
_____

family

a brother
_____
_____
_____

drink

_____
_____
_____
milk

Unit 12

A **Read and draw.**

Jim is a young footballer. What does he do every day?
Draw the times on the clocks.

1 I get up at quarter to seven.

2 I run at seven o'clock.

3 I go to school at ten to eight.

4 I get home at ten past four.

5 I play football at quarter past five.

6 I go to bed at half past nine.

Partner **B**, you are Jim.
Partner **A** ask questions.

| **A:** When do you get up? | **B:** At quarter to seven. |

Write about your day in your ET book.

B **Write the words.**

He's from Germany. He's German. He speaks German.
She's from Greece. She's Greek. She speaks Greek.
They're from Turkey. They're Turkish. They speak Turkish.
She's from France. She's <u>French</u>. She speaks French.

He's from _____. He's Italian. He speaks _____.

They're from _____. They're _____. They speak Spanish.

Write about you in your ET book.

46

Listen and write.

When are the programmes? Listen and write the times.

Your TV programmes today!

Channel 1   time

Yosemite Park   `4.30`

Tom and Jerry
(cartoon)   ` `

News   ` `

The Space Monster
(horror film)   ` `

Channel 2   time

Football
(Spain - Italy)   ` `

The Red Shoes
(musical)   ` `

News   ` `

Which programmes do the children want to watch? Tick the chart.

	Beth	Emma	Joe	Al	Tammy
Yosemite Park		✓			
Football					
Tom and Jerry					
The Space Monster					
The Red Shoes					

 Which programmes do your friends want to watch? Ask your class.
Write the answers in your ET book.

I want to watch...

Alessandra wants to watch...

D **Write the letters.**

1 It's on the football. G

2 It's in front of the goalkeeper. —

3 It's behind the goal. —

4 It's next to the referee. —

5 It's in the goal. —

6 It's behind the footballer. —

7 It's in front of the footballer. —

Which country is it? _____

E **Play a game.**

Draw these in your dungeon. Draw them *on*, *next to*, *behind*, *in front of* or *in* things. Hide your picture from your partner.

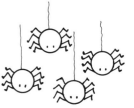

two bats   three mice   a ghost   four spiders

Where are the things in your dungeon? Partner **A**, tell **B**.

A: There's a mouse on the box . . . there are two spiders in front of the bed . . .

Partner **B**, draw **A**'s dungeon. Take it in turns.

48

your dungeon

your partner's dungeon

F **Say.**

Buzz, buzz, buzz, go the bees in the sun.
Buzz, buzz, buzz, making honey is fun!

Unit 13

A Listen and write.

What did they see?
Listen and tick the chart.

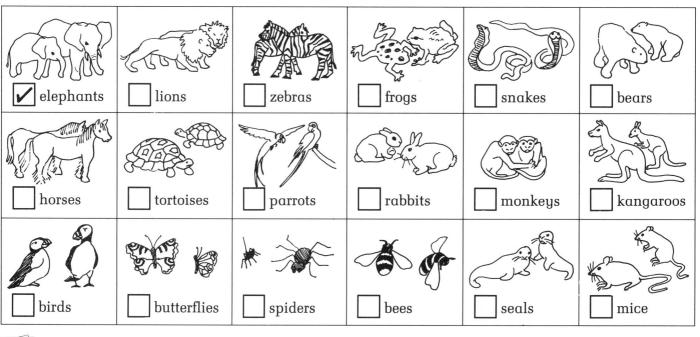

✓ elephants	☐ lions	☐ zebras	☐ frogs	☐ snakes	☐ bears
☐ horses	☐ tortoises	☐ parrots	☐ rabbits	☐ monkeys	☐ kangaroos
☐ birds	☐ butterflies	☐ spiders	☐ bees	☐ seals	☐ mice

Now write what the children saw on safari in your ET books like this:

On safari they saw
some elephants, some...
They didn't see any...

B Find the animals.

The words go this way → this way ← this way ↑ and this way ↓

e	l	e	p	h	a	n	t
f	i	l	i	o	n	a	o
r	o	e	b	r	m	r	r
o	n	p	e	s	i	b	t
g	s	h	a	e	s	e	o
b	e	a	r	b	e	z	i
e	a	n	e	k	a	n	s
e	l	t	o	i	l	r	e

Now write:
There are two zebras,

50

C **Ask your partner.**

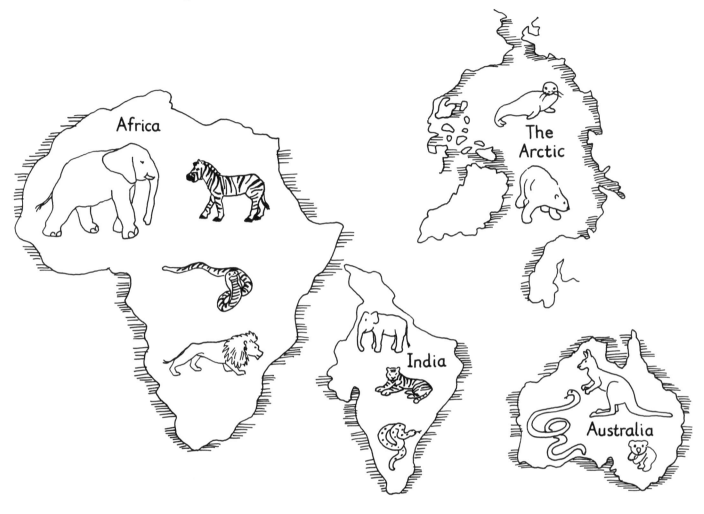

Look at the maps then ask your partner:

A: Are there any lions in India?
B: No. Are there any elephants in India?

Ask two questions about each country.
Then write in your ET book like this:

There are some lions and
elephants in Africa but
there aren't any seals.

Write about India, America and the Arctic in the same way.
Then write about the animals in your country.

D Write questions.

Choose an animal. Write six questions about it.
Give the questions to your partner.
Can you answer his/her questions?

lion

rabbit

snake

seal

1 What _____

2 Where _____

3 How _____

4 How many _____

5 Why _____

6 _____

What is your favourite animal? Write about it in your ET book.
Draw a picture.

E Choose and write.

What do these signs mean?

| Turn right.
Turn left.
Ride bikes here
Stop. | Don't turn right.
Don't turn left.
Don't ride bikes here.
Don't stop. | Be careful, rocks!
Be careful, elephants!
Be careful, horses! |

1 *Don't turn left.*

2 _____

3 _____

4 _____

5 _____

6 _____

F Choose the odd one out.

Find the odd one out in each box. Why is it different?

| **1** elephant
mouse
spider
bear | **2** monkey
kangaroo
elephant
zebra | **3** bear
rabbit
bee
butterfly | **4** parrot
butterfly
bee
frog |

Write in your ET books like this:

1 A spider, because an elephant, a mouse and a bear have four legs.

53

A **Look and read.**

Mary walks to school.

She goes to the cinema by bus.

She goes to London by train.

She goes to California by plane.

Now ask your partner.

How do you go to school?
               to your grandma's house?
               to the cinema?
               to a football match?
               to the sea?
               to the country?

Write about you and your partner in your ET book like this:

I walk to school. I go to my…		
Clara goes to school by…		

B **Look and write.**

The weather.

Today's weather.   Tomorrow's weather.

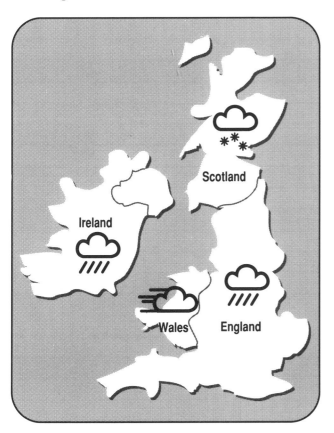 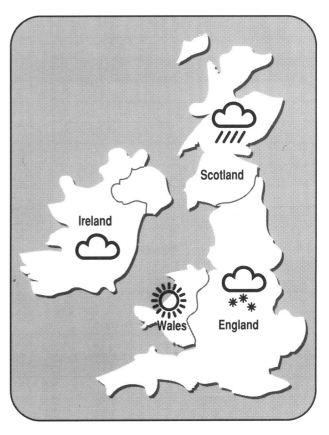

Write about the weather today and tomorrow.

In England _today it is raining._
Tomorrow it is going to snow.

In Scotland _____

_____

In Wales _____

_____

In Ireland _____

_____

 Now write about the weather today and tomorrow
in your country in your ET book.

C Listen and write.

Uncle Colin is going to have a goodbye party for
the children. He is making his shopping list.
Listen then tick what he is going to buy.

☐ sausages	☐ pizza	☐ paper
☐ chicken	☐ cake	☐ paper plates
☑ bread	☐ eggs	☐ paper cups
☐ sandwiches	☐ coffee	☐ balloons
☐ crisps	☐ tea	☐ video
☐ biscuits	☐ lemonade	☐ cassette
☐ ice cream	☐ hats	

Now write what Uncle Colin is going to buy, like this:
He's going to buy some bread.

And what Uncle Colin isn't going to buy, like this:
He isn't going to buy any crisps.

You are going to have a party. What are you going to buy?
Ask your partner. Write in your ET book.

D A Game. Do it!

1 Find a piece of paper.
Write:

Close one eye.	Smile.
Stand up.	Open your mouth.
Don't move.	Sit down.
Don't smile.	Make a funny face.

2 Cut the paper. Put the pieces of paper on the table.

3 Choose one piece of paper. Don't show your partner.

4 Read it. Do it. Your partner guesses.

What does it say on my paper?

Smile?

Yes. Your turn.

Unit 15

A **Look and say.**

1 What's the time by the clock in the kitchen?
2   by the clock in the dining room?
3   by the clock in the bathroom?
4   by the clock in the bedroom?
5   by the clock in the living room?

Now write.

1 <u>It's quarter past one.</u>

2 _____

3 _____

4 _____

5 _____

What's the time by your watch?

58

B **Read and write.**

These are pictures of Uncle Colin's family.
Read and then write their names under their pictures.

Aunt Kate

Aunt Kate has got short, fair hair. She wears specs. She always looks tired.
Uncle Bert hasn't got any hair. He's got a big nose.
Uncle Sam has got short, black hair. He always looks happy.
Uncle Fred wears specs. He's got big ears. He always looks sad.
Aunt Maude has black hair. She always looks angry.
Aunt Sally is very old. She always wears a hat.

In your ET book draw a picture of your aunt and uncle.
Then write about them.

C Look, read and write.

Al and Joe's favourite film is *Ghostbusters*.
Their favourite filmstar is Sigourney Weaver.
Here is her picture:

She has long, dark hair. Her eyes are
brown. She is very beautiful.

Stick a picture of your favourite filmstar in your
ET book. Write about him/her.

D Look and say.

There are seven ghosts hiding in the hall at Cliff Castle.
Where are they?

Now write in your ET book like this:

There's a ghost behind
the picture and a
ghost under...

E **Listen and write the words in the boxes.**

Here are the words for 'ghost' in five different languages.
How do you spell them? Listen and write the words in the boxes.

ghost				
English	Spanish	German	French	Italian

F **A game.**

Play the diamond game with your partner.

Think of a word in English (castle).
On a piece of paper draw a line for each letter like
this:

_ _ _ _ _ _

Your partner is going to guess the word.
He guesses a letter: 'a'?
Put the letter 'a' in the right place.

_ a _ _ _ _

He guesses again: 'p'?
There isn't a 'p' in your word. Start to draw a
diamond like this:

_ a _ _ _ _   P╱

He guesses again: 'o'?
There isn't an 'o'. Draw another line on your
diamond.

_ a _ _ _ _   P⋀o

When your partner guesses the word, he is the
winner.
When you draw three diamonds, you are the
winner.

c a _ _ _ e   P⬦o r⋁u
w⋀d y⋀b
n⋁g i⋁f

Key words and expressions

Unit 1
winter
Scotland
train
mountain
fun
windsurf
tree
in the holidays
by the sea
at home
in the mountains
in the country

Unit 2
castle
uncle
grandpa
cousin
aunt
England
Ireland
Wales
live
send
wall
door
window
clock
Come in.
Wait and see!

Scotland factfile
beautiful
high
deep
ski
kilt
bagpipes
dinosaur
neck
seal
scientist
extinct

Unit 3
Rooms in a house
living room
kitchen
dining room
bedroom
bathroom

toilet
hall
garden

stairs
upstairs
downstairs
want
bookshelf
button
press
go in
secret
giant
computer
key (computer)
happen
flat
What is it like?
in the town

Unit 4
type
space
new
planet
spaceship
seatbelt
pick up
key (door)
ring (n)
magic
chose
stood
about
Just a minute.

Space factfile
astronaut
water
keep fit
first
grow
thin
fat
web
pack
tray
magnet
oven
washbasin
hole
inside
soap

Unit 5
world
Earth
Africa
India
Australia
suddenly
saw
land (v)
had
rainbow
round (prep)
beautiful
flower
mushroom
teddy bear
doll
awful
noise
mouse/mice

Unit 6
more
found
machine
back (n)
took
made
camera
parrot
diary
Look and see!

Months
January
February
March
April
May
June
July
August
September
October
November
December

Inventions factfile
artist
litter
string
ring (v)

bell
driver
glue
wheel
stick
useful
sandwich
invent
chain
zip
famous
telephone
send
message

Unit 7
spell (v)
National Park
redwood
hundred
thousand
(11) years old
bear
over
through
bridge
eye test
pot
seed
plastic bag
Quick!

Unit 8
lights
kill
hit
hurt (adj)
fine
cinema
horror film
musical
adventure
comedy
cartoon
fortune-teller
turn over

Jobs
filmstar
doctor
engineer
pop singer
footballer

Look out!

Film tricks
factfile
real
models
glass
made of
sugar
break
blood

Unit 9
snow(y)
oil
fur
Rescue Centre
tanker
scarf
chase
laugh
can (n)
newspaper
litter
polar bear
future
pollution
Poor thing!

Unit 10
diamond
great grandmother
code
dungeon
message
clue
think
carpet
bus
toy
talk
tomorrow

Arctic
factfile
land
shine
midnight
cry
tears
freeze
sledge
thick
warm
reindeer
fox

hare
snowflake

Unit 11
past (n)
early
coal mine
all day
hard (adv)
push
at night
late
tired
gave
soup
a piece of
another
glad
lemonade
lock
stick (n)
moustache
beard
What's the matter?
Give it to me.

Unit 12
match
World Cup
Brazil
team
score
goal
talk
pass
fast
goalkeeper
wait
shoot
whistle
wonderful

Nationalities
Brazilian
Spanish
American
Italian
German
Greek
Turkish
French

from
speak
referee

get home
programme
channel
one-nil
one all
half time

Olympics
factfile
held
each
event
medal
gold
silver
bronze

Sports
athletics
boxing
cycling
basketball
gymnastics
swimming
skiing
skating
ski-jumping

other
won
became
point (n)
flag
mascot
last
athlete

Unit 13
safari
lion
zebra
elephant
sell
tusk
money
hear(d)
catch
dangerous
gun
hold/held
leaves (n)
leave (v)
ornament
a long way
Be careful!

Unit 14
safe
go back
everything
police
left
right
Oh dear!

Animals in danger
factfile
mammoth
dodo
hunter
hunt
crocodile
skin
law
rare
shopkeeper
prison
cut down
destroy
save
male
female

Unit 15
last
backwards
turn off
follow
disappear

Longman Group UK Limited,
Longman House, Burnt Mill, Harlow,
Essex CM20 2JE, England
and Associated Companies throughout the world.

First published 1992
ISBN 0 582 02065 4

Illustrated Nigel Alexander, Mike Gordon,
Helen Herbert, Jan Lewis, Raynor Design.

We are grateful to the following for permission to
reproduce copyright photographs:

FORMAT/Jacky Chapman for page 33 (right);
Picturepoint-London for page 9; St John Pope for page
33 (left, middle left & middle right) & Rex Features for
page 60.

Picture research by Sandie Huskinson-Rolfe
(PHOTOSEEKERS).

Designed by Raynor Design.

Set in Linotronic 300 Melior 14/16pt

Printed in Great Britain
by William Clowes Limited, Beccles and London